November Storm
Joshua Crocker

NOVEMBER STORM

ISBN: 979-8-9879131-4-7 (paperback)

Library of Congress Control Number: 2024925511

Cover design by Joshua Crocker.

Page design by Joshua Crocker.

Paperback print. First edition 2024.

Published by the Paragon Coalition.
Norman, OK
paragoncoalition.com

Dedicated to
Lady the Ladybug

Other Works by Joshua

One Day I'll Know
Snippets of Ink
Songs About Self-Defense
Oh No, Another Homemade Christmas Present

Table of Contents

waiting on a storm

I hate the feeling of waiting on a storm.
The anxiety builds in my stomach
for things I have little control over.
As I went to bed Halloween night,
I had the same feeling in my mind.
There's nothing like a November storm.

I feel nauseous, to be fair, I haven't been eating well.
Life has been more chaotic as of late,
there are tornadoes in the fall, voting lines have begun,
and I've been staying up way too late.
You can't rhyme 'late' with 'late'.
I'm worried over more things than I can count.
Sorry Jesus, but that whole 'Do-Not-Be-Anxious' thing
hasn't been working out for me.

The skies are uniquely gray, it's beautiful really.
The wind picks up the falling leaves
and scatters them around town.
I know this week will be a hectic one,
and the one after that will likely also be.
By the time Thanksgiving Day gets here
I don't even know what I'll be saying thanks for.

Some things just don't make sense to me.
People like me are praying for the country,
but we've been casting our ballots differently.
Wasn't it just last night we were all
hiding in our closets from a storm?
But then the very next day you go out
and cheer for something way worse.

A moment ago the sun peaked out from the clouds.
It hid away again soon after.
If that isn't a metaphor for something, what is.
I'm even fearful of the things that make me happy.
Like that nervous feeling you get around a pretty girl.
I've been trying to impress this woman
who probably just sees me as a friend.
I want to make her laugh, but I keep stuttering instead.
When I smiled the other day, did anyone notice?
Most of all, did she notice?
Or like the sun, do I hide away too soon?

I'm sitting in the dark, waiting on a storm.
Trying to write some words that reflect how I feel.
Why should I worry over the things I can't control?
I don't pray as much as I should.
Or maybe my prayers are just misunderstood.
I've walked more miles to nowhere than I'm aware of.
The rain has begun to fall from above,
and I feel anxious of what's to come.
I keep walking down the street regardless,
preparing my thoughts for the month ahead.
Thoughts of hope and dread.
There's nothing like a November storm.

Friendships on Hold

Where did you go?
Let me just say, it's true.
You don't realize what you got, till you don't.
One, two, three, probably more.
While you're drowning in homework and job applications,
I'm drowning my feelings in music.
We've got so much to talk about,
but you don't have the time to be my therapist.
And I'd rather complain than solve the issue.
I look for you when I go for walks,
I'm still waiting for a text back,
we never did find a time to grab drinks.
One, two, three, probably more.
Is it too cliché to say I miss you?
What's worse, I don't know if I do.
Were we ever all that close?
Did I ever actually think about you
outside of the context of myself?
I don't know if I ever really did.
After a couple days of not seeing you, I moved on.
Did it even take you that long?
One, two, three, probably more, friendships on hold.

After 9:30 I start to get a little delirious.
Maybe I'll zone out or doze off a bit.
I'm not built for college late nights.
Or maybe I'm just not built for real life.
The pressure is too much for me.

When I reread this in the morning it will be nonsense.
I haven't been thinking right all day,
and all the nervousness has broken me.
When I try to remember what I said or who I am,
all I know is the memories won't reflect the same.

I think you've gotten a little delirious too.
While I sit here quietly losing my mind,
you outwardly are losing all sense of sanity.
I can sit back and watch, I laugh, but inside I'm not.
Because my eyes can only see what my head says it can.

The clock ticks closer to 10:00, and I'm a little delirious.
Nothing makes sense anymore, did it ever really?
My imagination hates me more than anyone else does.
I should just accept I'm my own worst enemy.
The pressure is just too much for me.

I Want to Believe

I want to believe that God's people are good.
Jesus, I want to believe that you loved everyone,
but my brothers and sisters don't seem to think so.
I want to go to church and sing songs of grace,
not question if I belong in these worship halls.
I don't need all the facts, that ain't my style,
I just need something to believe in,
and I need y'all to believe in me.

I want to believe that all prayers are heard.
Jesus, I want to believe that you live still,
but the words my friends read are increasingly shallow.
I want to go to church and learn about spirituality,
not pretend to be the same as I was at seventeen.
I don't understand why we can't have real conversations,
but instead must justify everything through old scrolls,
none of us willing to think any differently.

I want to believe. I want to believe in the stories.
I want to believe in God's love.
I want to believe all people can have a voice.
I want to believe. I want to believe this can be my home.

All It Takes

All it takes is a smile and compliment
and I know I'm screwed.
It's been a week now and I'm still not sure what to do.
I won't say I'm crushing,
but that would explain the blushing.
I keep doing this to myself, so here we go again.
You called me smart,
but I'm dumb when it comes to the heart.
I keep glancing your way; you're just nice to look at.
There's no way this ends well,
but there's only one way to tell.
I'm trying to find the right words to say, but hey,
maybe a smile and conversation with you is all it takes.

There's so much to say
that I don't know where to begin

I could write for hours   *i tend to*
but I'll stare at a blank screen instead

It feels   like
I'm walking through the fog,
and I'm not lost,

just confused

I'm questioning

my faith
the time of day
who I am
my own thoughts

a lot of things

Sleep has become a blessing
not a commodity

Restless at night   Restless during the day

And the worst part is

I love it

this is what I've been writing about

I don't care about the meaning,

just the theatrics

things could be terrible, but at least they're alive

poets are fueled by stories
that they can twist and turn
until they've lost all feeling

they're just words
and words are just memories

but when they ask me where I've been

I can tell them I've been walking in the fog

I just fear

that the fog will swallow me up

before I reach
the other side

but for now, I'm going to keep pace,
rummaging for a lighter

and if I can find a flame to follow
then the fog is no more than a brush with the sky

SADNESS

Walking down University Boulevard
is a girl with a sadness in her eyes.
Her blank stare tells more than enough.
She's not angry or mad or even upset,
just sad, unsure of what comes next.

Her eyes express a brokenness deep inside.
Last night something in her heart had died.
She had been fighting for so long,
but still lost in the end.
Worse than any loss,
was the truth she now believed.
She had always said people were inherently good,
this truth she had held for so long was now gone.
Her faith in humanity had vanished in her sleep.

Her eyes give way to a thousand words.
A prayer of mourning for her sisters,
for words that would never be enough.
A poem of sorrow for herself,
for her existence had been denied.

There's a girl with a sadness in her eyes.
No tears, no words to say.
She knew she would never be the same.
Her heart wrote the eulogy for her younger self,
the girl who had still believed in goodness.
What comes next is still uncertain.
I hope she keeps fighting,
finds a way to heal the sadness in her eyes.

Sitting in the Dark

I was lying in bed this morning, counting down
the seconds until my phone told me to get up.

When the alarm finally went off, I begrudgingly
got up and checked my notifications.

About ten minutes earlier my town was under a
tornado warning, and I hadn't heard a thing.

Why are these times so strange?
Humans are acting more like robots
and the robots are more humanlike.
There are April showers in November
and I just keep sitting in the dark.

I got up and turned on the news, muting it
while I prepared myself some breakfast.

I drove to a nearby coffee shop to work on this book,
but as I opened my word doc, the power went out.

Now I'm here, surrounded by a handful of other people,
writing alone in a dimly lit room.

Why are these times so strange?
Humans are acting more like robots
and the robots are more humanlike.
There are April showers in November
and I just keep sitting in the dark.

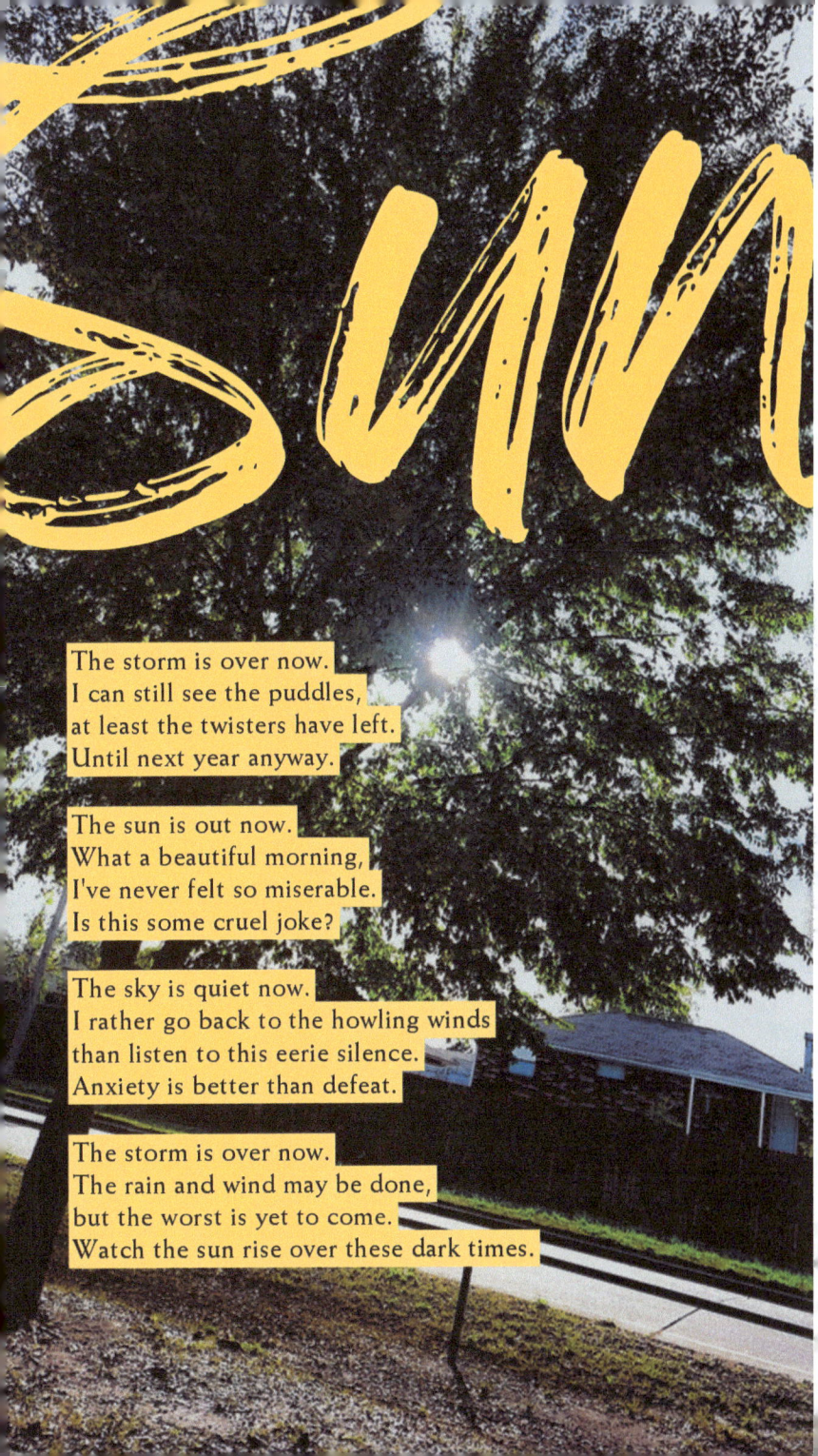

The storm is over now.
I can still see the puddles,
at least the twisters have left.
Until next year anyway.

The sun is out now.
What a beautiful morning,
I've never felt so miserable.
Is this some cruel joke?

The sky is quiet now.
I rather go back to the howling winds
than listen to this eerie silence.
Anxiety is better than defeat.

The storm is over now.
The rain and wind may be done,
but the worst is yet to come.
Watch the sun rise over these dark times.

Sad Stuff

So, I was talking with my cousin.
Told her I was writing a book.
She asked me about what.
I said sad stuff.
And she was like, why sad stuff?
And I was like, why not?
It's funny how much I enjoy the misery.
She was like, you're weird.
And I was like, well thank you.

I've been known for a few things,
one being I can be a little dramatic.
I act all traumatic, I'm playing it up.
I'm not lying, per say, just embellishing.

So, I was talking with my cousin.
She asked if I'm okay.
I said I've never been better.
I was like, you want to hear something sad?
And she was like, why would I?

Let's also get one thing clear,
most of the stories aren't even that sad.
Half of these pages are just ramblings
about my family, crushes, and a pet ladybug.
But who cares about that?
I just care about the sad stuff.

So, I was talking with my cousin.
I said writing about sad stuff makes the stuff seem less sad.
She was like, and how is that?
And I was like, I always seem to tie it back to hope.
And she was like, well I would hope you do.
I've been known for a few things,
one being my unrelenting optimism.
She was like, I still love you, but you're kinda weird.
And I was like, well I wouldn't want it any other way.

Isolationism

I'm an introverted kind of person.
I like to have time to myself.
I still feel lonely from time to time though.
It's not just that I miss my friends,
but more that I feel like I'm taking on life alone.
There will be someone who reads this
who feels the same away.
Here's what I want you to know:
You're not in this alone.
I've seen the sadness in people's eyes.
I hear the fear in your voices.
I've seen tornado wreckage before,
I've watched the streets begin to flood,
but the worst feeling when a storm is near
is knowing I'm alone with nowhere to go.
When the storm of our life is on the way,
don't let yourself feel isolated.
My theory is that the people that hate you
want you to feel alone, they want you scared.
In a system of isolationism
you're more likely to fall in line.
Don't give in. Don't hide.
And maybe I'm not the one to give this advice.
I've spent the entire year doing just this.
I was angry at people I shouldn't have been.
But y'know what, it didn't help.
I've realized I'm happier when I let people love me.
A thing that seems obvious to me now.
So, when a storm is near, don't isolate yourself.
You weren't made to take on life alone.
Let yourself be happy still. Let yourself be loved.
It won't make the storm go away,
but it'll make the wind feel more like a breeze.

Distracted
A Collection of Loose Thoughts

Damnit, I've been a bit distracted lately.

I've been bringing my dreams with me when I wake,

tired from all the hem and hawing as I'm toss and turning.

Can't even finish a simple task without getting a little sidetracked.

I guess I'm not complaining though.

I told myself in the moment I wouldn't overthink this,

but I've been playing another round of

my favorite game, 'Is She Being Friendly or Flirting?'

The answer is always there's no way to tell.

That won't stop me from replaying the footage on loop.

The way you smiled and rubbed my shoulder

and the stupid ways I find to make a fool of myself.

It's all the time. I'm habitual overanalyzer,

too quick to write love stories in my mind,

too slow to say the words I already designed.

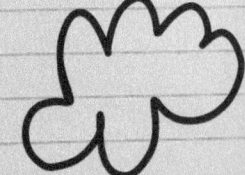

I write some things down.

I claim these feelings will make for a great book.

I don't know if that's true.

These poems are less art, more me decompressing.

Why do you have to be so distracting?

I guess I have always been one to get

distracted by something pretty.

Social Hangover

Did you sleep well last night?
Well, I could have slept worse.
Feeling hungover without ever taking a drink.
Drinking away what should have been a great time.
I've always thought I didn't have the social battery
to be around people for a long time,
but maybe I don't have the mental capacity
to eat breakfast alone the next morning.
My mind races, completely overthinking.
Thinking through every damn thing.
Every time I touch the memories
they turn a little more blue.
But none of that's even true.
As soon as I roll out of bed I let the TV think for me.
Open a jar of peanut butter to help heal me.
Did you have fun last night?
Funny enough, I don't even know.
Anytime I let my heart start beating,
the next day it'll be head that's beating.

NOT ENOUGH

I mumbled my words when I said you were cute.
It seems the awkward glances only go one way.
This could be something more, but I've already
decided if I ask you out, you'll just say no.

If I were just a little funnier, you would laugh more,
and if I was just a little hotter, you would be blushing.
If I was just a little better, then maybe. But I'm not.

I'm not enough for you.
I'm not strong enough, I'm not tall enough.
There's nothing that makes me special.
I'm not clever enough, I'm not charming enough.
At least I'm not stupid enough to think you
think about me the same way I think about you.

Sitting at the girl's table listening to them talk smack.
'No offense,' you say. Don't patronize me.
I'm glad you remembered I was here,
cause it seems I have a tendency to be invisible
until I decide to make a fool of myself.

Go back to being a happily alone doll in denial.
This constant 'will she, won't I' makes you sound senile.

I'm better at being a brother than a boyfriend,
that's where my experience is at.
I make a great side character in any friend group,
but I shouldn't fool myself into thinking
I'll ever be the star. Cause I'm not.

If I were just a little funnier, you would laugh more,
and if I was just a little hotter, you would be blushing.
If I was just a little better, then maybe. But I'm not.

I'm not enough for you.
I'm not strong enough, I'm not tall enough.
There's nothing that makes me special.
I'm not clever enough, I'm not charming enough.
At least I'm not stupid enough to think you
think about me the same way I think about you.

Now it's my turn to say, 'no offense.'
What makes a girl like you so worth this beatdown?
Whenever I try to imagine us together,
I can only ever see my worst qualities.
In frustration, I yell back at the voices in my head,
but deep down I know I'm telling myself
exactly what I want to hear.

You're not enough. You'll never be enough.
You're just a loser with loser feelings too.
You're not enough. You'll never be enough.
Enough of a friend. Enough of a man.
Enough of a human being.
You're just a rough draft of someone else.
And that'll never be enough.

It doesn't matter what you say.
I've already told myself I'm not enough.

The Need to Apologize

Dear Jenna, I feel the need to apologize.
For what, I don't know why.
I know you're not mad at me.
In fact, you've been nothing but kind.
But Jenna, I've been too hard on myself lately.
It's cliché, yet I feel tugged in every direction.
I'm obsessed with the people and things
that don't seem to be worth my time.
Jenna, I'm sorry. I don't want to let you down.
It seems the more I write, the more I forget.
I'm too smart to just let myself fall apart.
But I'm too young to do anything else.

Dear Joshua, do you know I love you?
It seems you forget that too often.
When I see you, I just feel compassion.
I know how tiring these days have been for you.
But Joshua, you can't keep hating yourself.
You say you don't, but I hear the way you talk.
Let yourself be happy with the people and things
that surround you, just stop obsessing over time.
Joshua, it'll be okay. You're not going to let me down.
The more we walk together, the more we understand.
Don't let me or anyone else take over your life.
We're too young to know everything.

Dear Jenna, I feel I've been lying to you.
Maybe worse, I abandoned you.
I've been lying to everyone, most of all myself.
I rather fantasize about my little stories.
Jenna, it seems I've lost the plot.

Dear Joshua, I see through all the nonsense.
You know I'm not going anywhere.
I think the worst lie you've told yourself
is that you have to choose what happens next.
Joshua, life is more complex than one story.

Dear Jenna, can I be vulnerable with you?
I don't know how to keep up with all this.
I never thought real life would be so complicated.
I've been writing in overtime to process it all.
Jenna, I've been struggling lately.

Dear Joshua, I'll always be there for you.
Who said you had to keep up with all this?
Real life isn't a battle to win, it's a journey.
Your words are better said than kept away.
Joshua, it's okay to struggle. That's just a part of life.

BUSY BODY

Deadlines will be the death of me.
Meetings, videos to edit, pages to revise.
Please don't forget to DM me in the morning.
Once you're done eating breakfast
it'll be time for lunch.
Didn't have time to shave again,
forgot to click save and send.
Creative projects are fun till they're not.
I love being productive, but I hate being busy.

AN OUTLANDISH REQUEST

I just wanted to live without fear.
Was I too demanding?
Was it unfair of me to expect more from you all?
I would take a compromise.
I would even admit I was wrong at times,
but this means more than petty disagreements.
Is this the best we can do?
I just wanted to protect my family and friends.
In the future, how will I explain this to my kids?
Is this lying, racism, and stupidity
really represent who we are?
I thought we were smarter than that?
Maybe I was the one who was ignorant all along.
Give me anyone, give me anything,
just don't give me a hateful, spiteful, evil dirtbag.
Is that too much to ask?

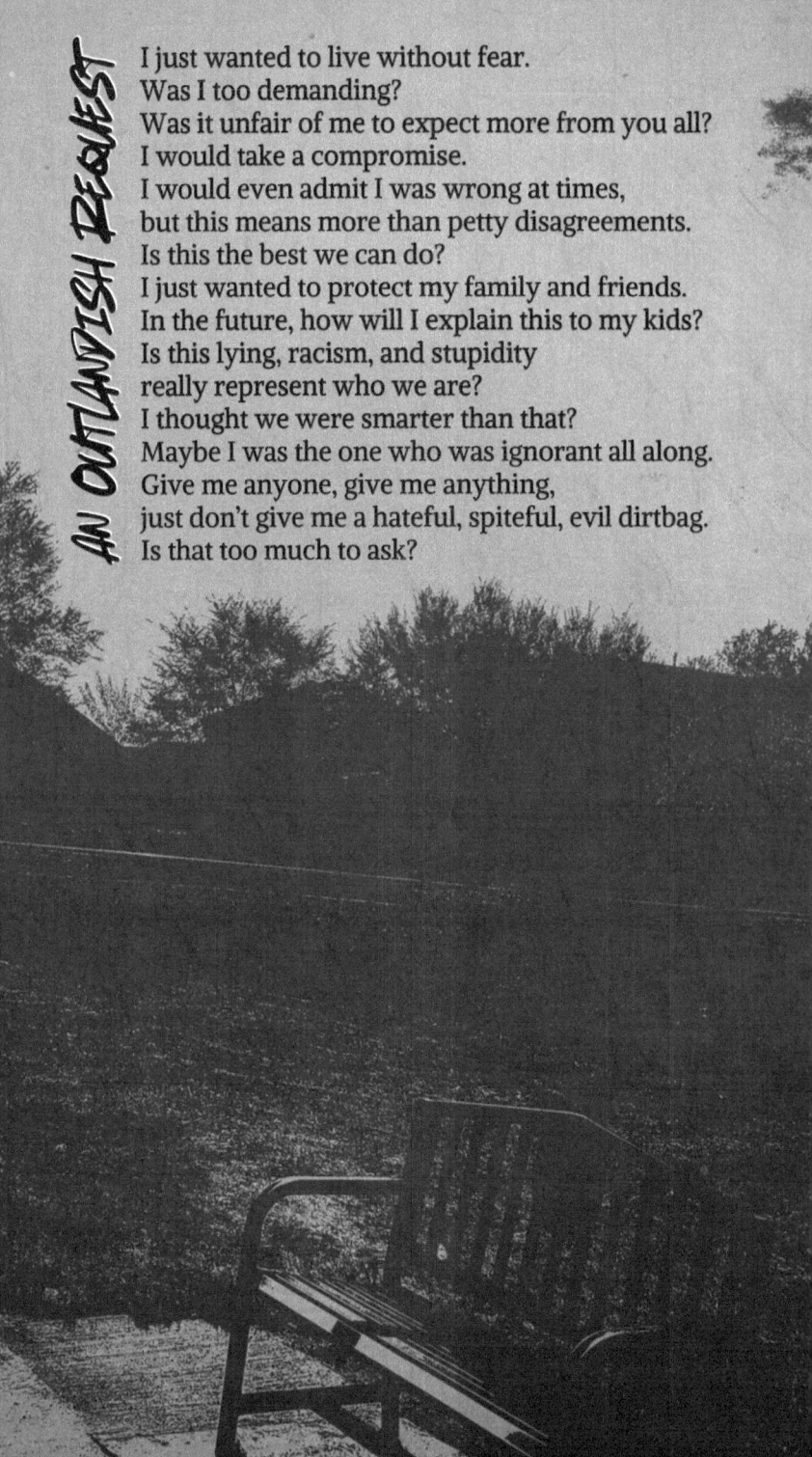

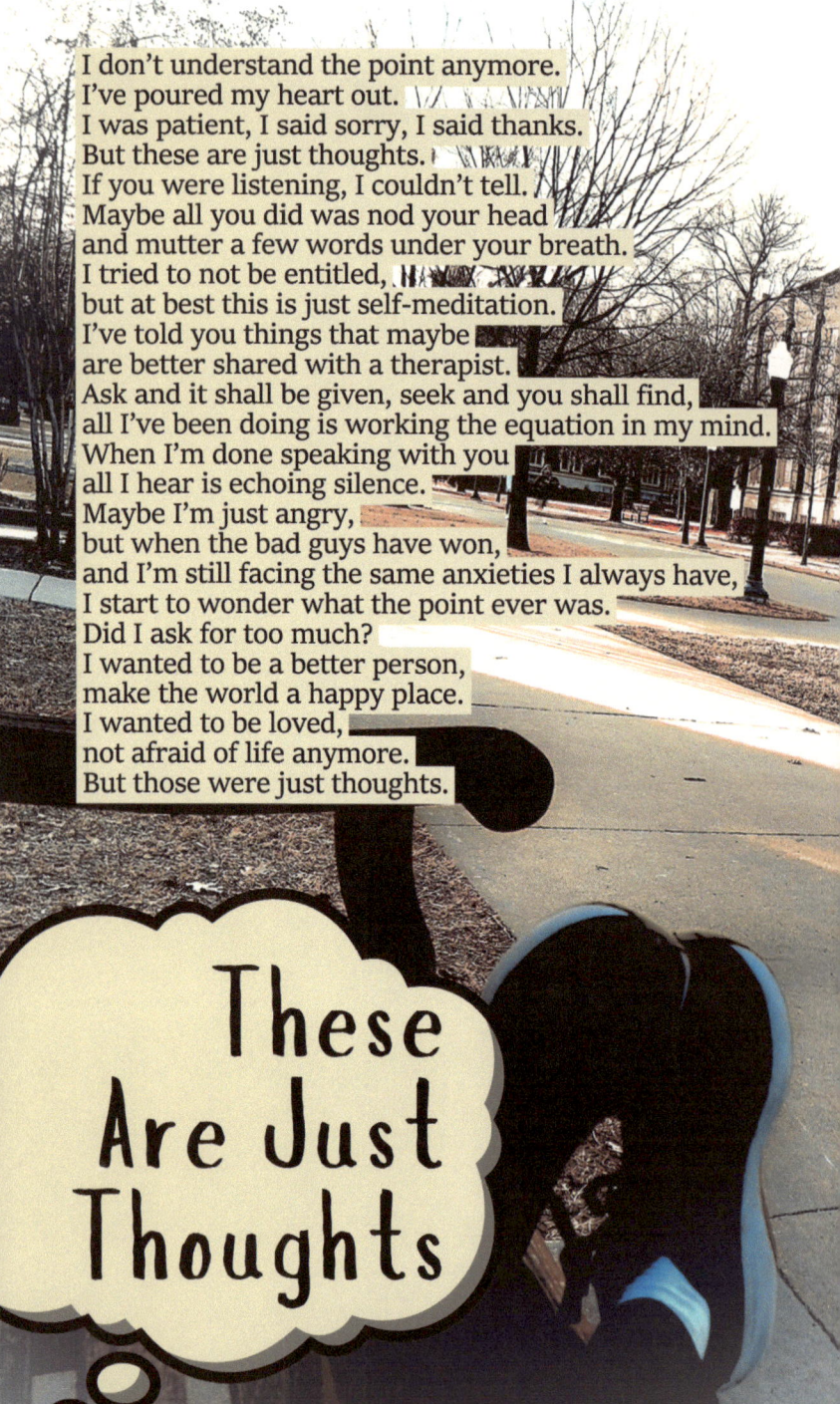

I don't understand the point anymore.
I've poured my heart out.
I was patient, I said sorry, I said thanks.
But these are just thoughts.
If you were listening, I couldn't tell.
Maybe all you did was nod your head
and mutter a few words under your breath.
I tried to not be entitled,
but at best this is just self-meditation.
I've told you things that maybe
are better shared with a therapist.
Ask and it shall be given, seek and you shall find,
all I've been doing is working the equation in my mind.
When I'm done speaking with you
all I hear is echoing silence.
Maybe I'm just angry,
but when the bad guys have won,
and I'm still facing the same anxieties I always have,
I start to wonder what the point ever was.
Did I ask for too much?
I wanted to be a better person,
make the world a happy place.
I wanted to be loved,
not afraid of life anymore.
But those were just thoughts.

These Are Just Thoughts

Angry Acquaintance Phase

At best we exchange awkward small talk,
with nothing much to chat about.
We used to go on and on forever.
What happened to change that?

You used to be someone I could trust in,
you were my family, my friends,
but that has come to an end.
I no longer believe in you.
We loved each other, at least we pretended to.
But just because I knew you when I was a kid
doesn't mean I have to follow after you.
I have enough evidence to know
you don't really care about me.
You were my family, my friends,
now we're just acquaintances passing by.

The words don't add up.
You contradict yourself in every conversation.
We may smile and greet each other to keep peace,
but what was the last real thing we said to one another?
It's not my fault I've matured
while you've stayed the same.

You used to be someone I could trust in,
you were my family, my friends,
but that has come to an end.
I no longer believe in you.
I'm not trying to say anyone is at fault here,
I think you and I are just fundamentally different people.
So, can we just let this go?
Stop believing a lie, pretending we still get along.
You were my family, my friends,
now we're just acquaintances passing by.

God Above

Have you turned away from this wicked place yet?
Forsaken us like we've forsaken you.
You gave us dominion over the seas and sky,
why is it everything we touch seems to die?
Do you stay away because your creation
has become too powerful and destructive?

God above,
do certain people deserve to live on the street?
My love,
can more bombs really lead to peace?
God above,
are our bodies made to be a prison cell?
My love,
does our endless pain really serve us well?

God, what would you say about us?
If you hadn't given your word,
would you send another flood?
How long is it before we cause
our own extinction event?
It only took two generations before
we learned to kill each other;
now we've learned to kill everything.

God above,
do certain people deserve to die alone?
My love,
what is kindness if it is not shown?
God above,
are our hearts meant to betray fate?
My love,
does our endless shouting reach heaven's gate?

I once believed no matter their faith
you made humans in good faith.
We were supposed to be a loving race,
but I think if there was proof without
a shadow of doubt that you were real,
our first reaction would be to build a weapon
so powerful that we could kill God himself.

I don't understand why,
why you haven't left us for good.
Is it just a sunk cost fallacy?
What promise do you still see in us?
Please tell me, because I don't see it.
It seems to me hate is stronger than love.
God above,
are we really the best life has to show?

Some days I dream of the places I'll run away to
on the day I leave you all behind.
I'll live in a place where it's freezing cold in November
and I won't have to worry about thunderclouds.
The bitter autumn wind as frigid as I am.
I won't even say goodbye.
Just pack up and skip town.
You won't even know why.
I won't talk much about my past.
Too proud to admit I miss my home.

Some days I don't think I'll be missed much
when I finally stop talking to you.
I could count on one hand the reasons to stay,
with the other hand in a guard as I back away.
I'll cut ties with all my friends,
caring about y'all was just too much.
The only number I'll keep is Izzy's,
text her when I miss my old life.
I'll tell mom to not worry when I send her a letter,
my new address on the envelope.
You can come and visit whenever you want.
Maybe I'll mail dad a copy of my next book,
my picture staring at you on the cover.
You can read it or not, whatever you want.

Some days I want to get as far away as I can,
a place where I'll be able to forget about it all.
I often pay more attention to the press
than what's actually in front of me.
I start to say things I never really meant.
I don't know if I'm frustrated or overwhelmed.
This is all too little; this can't be all life has to offer.
There has to be a place out there better than this.

Some days I might wonder if I was too hasty
back on the day I decided to leave it all behind.
If I ever return home no one will recognize me.
It'll have been ten, twenty years,
and I'll hardly look the same.
As I walk the same streets I did at nineteen,
I won't even know what to feel.
Nostalgia, hate, or regret.
I don't want to know.
This place was never the same without me.

Some days it feels I'm counting down the days
until I finally get up and run away.
Pack my laptop, clothes, and everyday necessities.
I'll send my black belt, books, and Peter Pan doll
in a box to my new residence.
Life was just too much and too little here.
I care too much about these streets.
I think too much about where the ends meet.
I'd rather just run away from it all,
not have to think about it anymore.
I seem too little to roll with the punches.
I feel too little inside when I pray next to you.
I'd rather just run away from you all,
not have to think about you anymore.

Some days I just want to run away,
you know in that scared way I always get
whenever faced with the realities of life.
I'm so afraid of so many things,
and it seems so easy to just flee.
I think, deep down, I know I'll never do it.
Past my fears, I'm not ready to say goodbye.
Life can seem so hard some days,
but this is still my home.
And I'm not going anywhere.

Vague

SITTING IN THE ART GALLERY IS A PIECE DEEMED ABSTRACT.
IS IT COWARDICE OR INSPIRED THAT THE ARTIST
LEFT THEIR NAME ANONYMOUS?
A MASTERPIECE OF THE READER'S CREATION.
IT COMES ACROSS AS PRETENTIOUS AND PRESUMPTUOUS,
AN UNDERLYING FEAR OF ONE'S NUMBNESS.

I'VE LEFT THE POEMS AND STORIES FAIRLY VAGUE.
YOU CAN'T OFFEND THOSE YOU DON'T SPEAK DIRECTLY TO.
I SAID THIS WOULD BE MY MOST HONEST PIECE YET,
BUT THERE'S NOTHING HERE.
THE UNNAMED VICTIMS OF MY STORYTELLING
ARE NOTHING MORE THAN CREATIONS OF MY IMAGINATION.

I SAID I WOULDN'T GET POLITICAL,
IS THAT BECAUSE I'VE REALIZED I DON'T STAND FOR ANYTHING?
I PROMISED TO NOT BE CRUDE,
IS THAT BECAUSE I FEAR PEOPLE DON'T LIKE ME ENOUGH ALREADY?
I REFUSE TO BE PERSONAL,
IS THAT BECAUSE I CAN'T HANDLE THE VULNERABILITY?

PAINT A SELF-PORTRAIT THE WAY YOU WANT THEM TO SEE IT.
LEAVE OUT THE BLEMISHES THAT DON'T COMPLY WITH LIFE.
REWRITE AND REWRITE UNTIL THE WORDS ARE WITHOUT MEANING.
HIDE YOUR TRUE FEELINGS IN THE PAGES NO ONE READS.
WHEN I GIVE THIS BOOK TO YOU AS A GIFT
I DON'T WANT IT TO BE THE LAST ONE I GIVE YOU.
BUT NOW IT'S JUST ANOTHER KNICK-KNACK
COLLECTING DUST IN THE CORNER OF YOUR ROOM.
THE WORDS ENTIRELY TOO VAGUE, THE MEANING UNCLEAR,
AN UNFORTUNATE REPRESENTATION OF WHO I AM TO YOU.

Lies, Eyes, and My Disguise

I say, "I'm not hungry. I ate before I arrived."
These are the words I repeat so many times.
What is true when all you see is fictionalized?

I say, "I hope you have a great rest of your week."
Tonight we both seemed rather quiet and meek.
I had more I wanted to say, like to ask if you're okay.

"Hey, I never realized how skinny you are," they say.
I don't know whether to say thanks or walk away.
There isn't a problem if I just ignore the signs.

They laugh, "Oh, it's you. I thought you were a girl."
Well, none of us are anything in this changing world.
What else did you expect me to say in return?

"You're so pretty," I say, but only inside my head.
I don't say it aloud, my eyes just follow you instead.
What is a lie if it's always by omission?

They say, "Are you hungry? You haven't eaten in a while."
These are the words repeated to me without a smile.
What am I so afraid of that I feel the need to hide?

Jupiter *and*
Saturn

Jupiter eyes Saturn from across galaxy waves.
Her rings glow in the starlight,
luminating her face in the sky's night.
He hides behind his satellites,
afraid his mind isn't on right.

Gravity pulls them around,
friends of the mighty sun.
The two pass by on their paths,
Jupiter hums and Saturn laughs,
her beauty in the sky is unmatched.
He aches from his core around her,
full of nervous gas and shaky ground.
Jupiter eyes Saturn from across galaxy waves.
She's brighter than a star in the night sky,
but he's just a rock floating right by.

Afterthought

I have a list of people who mean a lot to me.
The people who I think about all the time.
Even when I'm bored or tired, they're still on my mind.

How often do you think of me?
Call this fear irrational, people say the same about me,
but I fear I care more about you than you do me.
You only want to hang out when it's convenient for you.
I'm not demanding you to carve time
out of your busy schedule for me,
but it would be nice if you went a little
bit out of your way occasionally.
Or at the least, say hi to me.
Why should I always have to be the one
to initiate a conversation?
Am I just an extra on the set of your life?
Because that's how it feels.
I get it, you have problems you're dealing with, so do I.
But on your priority list, I don't even make the top 25.
I think about you all the time,
do you know that?
Do you even give me a passing thought?
If so, it doesn't feel like it.

I tend to say I think too much,
but why don't you think of me at all?
You mean the world to me,
but to you, I'm just an afterthought.

ILLOGICAL

I was only loosely paying attention in school,
now remind me what four plus three equals?
Is it an eight or a seven?

I was only loosely paying attention in church,
now remind me what the meaning of life is?
Can I create my own heaven?

I don't know.

It's illogical to think without breathing.
You'll pass out. I thought that was obvious.

My ideas and schemes are more insane by the day.
It's like refusing to get paid for all your hard work.
The thespian who can't tell reality from a work of fiction.
It's like listening to the same songs till they lose meaning.
The lesbian who tries to pick up girls at a Bible study.
It's like doing math and expecting the answer to change.

Is this insanity or a logical fallacy?
My heart has decided to ignore my brain
if it doesn't like what it has to say.

What's the point of baking a cake that you can't eat?
Okay, I lied. I don't even like cake.

I act like it's illogical to breathe without thinking.
No wonder I'm so tired all the time.
It's like thinking that a falling tree doesn't make a sound.

It's just illogical.

Compliments

I have this weird conundrum where the more I care about someone,
the harder it is to show them.
I've said so many nice things about you in my head,
but can never seem to compliment you when I should.
Am I incapable of encouragement if I'm not being paid for it?
Because it's starting to seem the only way I know
how to be personable is through martial arts.

Have I ever actually told my mom how much I look up to her?
Do I ever tell my dad I love him except when I'm leaving?
The only time I get close to people
is when I'm throwing them to the ground.
Do my brothers know how much I enjoy hanging out together?
Do my sisters realize I'd be there whenever they need me?
It's so much easier to be encouraging
after I get done kicking a person in the head.
I don't think I ever say thank you to my friends anymore.
I've never actually told a girl I find her pretty before.
It took me an entire hour to work up
the words to just say I like your jacket.

I have this weird conundrum where I forget
you can't read my thoughts about you.
I think so highly of so many people,
but I don't know if that always comes across clearly.
Am I incapable of complimenting people without a joke?
Because it's starting to seem the only way I know
how to be personable is through rambling poetry.

I have this tendency to think instead of speaking.
I think I like to overcomplicate being human.
I just hope I can learn to compliment people more.

Hey, I'm glad you're here, you look nice today.

Ladybug

Love and loss seem to me to be intrinsically tied.
I've spent years trying to avoid having my heart broken.
I'm so scared of being sad, I tried to burn any feeling at all.
This is an ode to a ladybug, my Lady.

My relationship with the truth is contentious at best.
I've always said poets are the kings of lying.
Real life is far too much for me to handle,
I'd rather only ever tell a story,
because then I get to choose how it ends.

If I'm honest with you, let you how I'm feeling,
I run the risk of you leaving.
Instead, let's just stay in a state of casual familiarity,
where the way we feel isn't quite clear.
You can't be hurt if you never get close to anything.

I didn't know how to handle losing you so soon.
Took me years to treat it as anything more than a cruel joke.
I've forgotten more people than I remember.
It seems every year I lose touch with another friend.
I don't see the point in getting close if they all leave eventually.

I've been trying to only ever live in the story I write,
all the while forgetting to live my life.
I'm done being afraid to leave my house,
afraid of losing the things that I care about.
If you do leave, I at least want you to know I loved you.
And if you stay, we can write this story together.

Growing older is learning to let go.
To a ladybug, my Lady, love to you.

Cruce to Santa Fe

I said a prayer last night.
The words were all over the place,
just like I seem to be.
I promise I wasn't mad,
hopefully I didn't come across that way.
I said some things,
I said I believe.
Or at least I'm choosing to.
I asked if you believe in me.
Because it's become hard to believe in myself.
I couldn't even remember my name.
But that's not what I was praying about.
I want to be patient and at peace with life.
Honest and confident in my thoughts.
I've run out of words,
but I was told you know my heart.
There's a divide between my soul and my actions.
How do I bridge the two?
I was told you are the master of timing.
Maybe the pieces are just lining up.
But I fear that I'll just ignore when they do,
not because I don't believe,
but because I don't believe in myself.
I really wish I did.
I want patience and peace.
I want honesty and confidence.
I want to believe in...

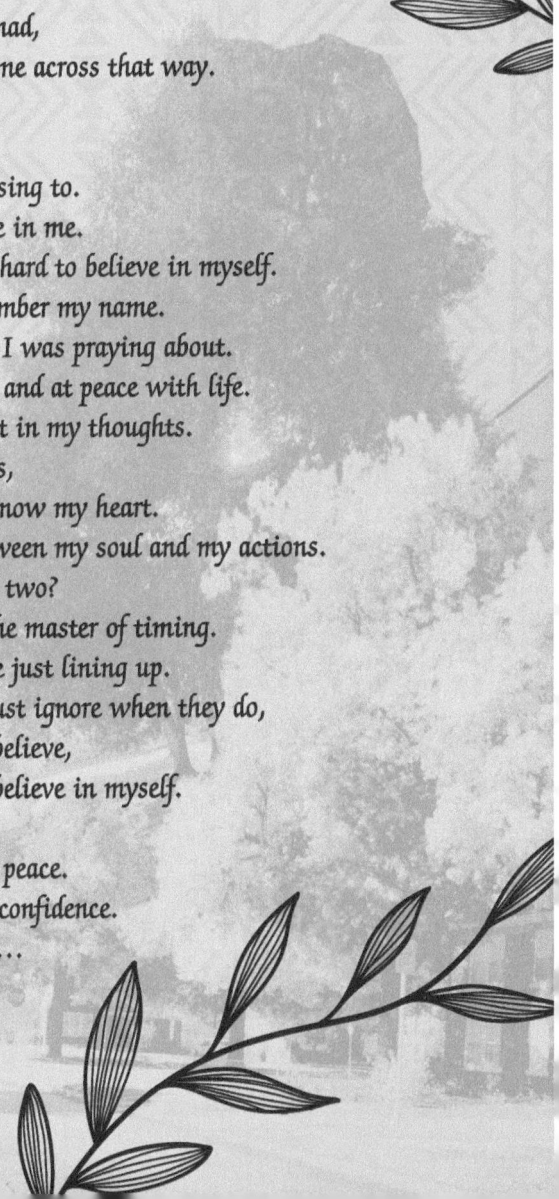

Hang With Me Here, I Can't Afford Therapy So I Write Instead

I overheard a lady talking. Two strangers having brunch next to me. And, frankly, it was none of my business. But she said something that sounded familiar to me. So, before I put my earbuds in, I listened in for a moment. Said something about the way she grew up. She didn't go into detail, but I could instantly connect the dots.

I grew up in the perfect family. That's what my parents told me. The illusion dropped eventually. If you had a problem, no you didn't. If you were feeling sad, try not feeling sad. I was the eldest, the golden child. They told me to speak my mind, but then everyone would realize I wasn't made of gold, but more of a copper alloy.

I've always had a lot on my mind. As a kid I would always tell people everything I was thinking, but then they told me to shut up. I don't know who *they* are, just the vague entity of the people around me. I felt embarrassed that I was inconveniencing people with the random thoughts in my head that really only made sense in the context of my head. Now I don't talk as much. Not in the same way, at least. Close friends will still say I'm always talking, but maybe that's because they never stop listening. Thank you for that, I get tired of only writing words for myself.

I'll never tell a kid they're mature for their age. The only difference between a well-spoken child and the class clown is one is afraid of being made a fool. Ask me how I know. I'm the smart one. I'm the mysterious one. I'm the quiet one. And emotional intelligence only gets you so far if you don't know how to speak your mind.

She keeps berating me for not eating anything. Says I'll fly away like a kite. Who's to say I haven't already? I'm not hungry. I'll eat later. You'll see me by the drink table. I always have a beverage in hand. And I'm always holding in my pee. Afraid if I step out for a moment, people will forget I was there to begin with. Do you want to know the truth? The part of the story I don't explain because I'm afraid it'll make me look bad. Whenever I'm around people, my body just shuts down. I'm too anxious to eat. Just the thought of food makes me begin to gag. I should really see someone about it, but I treat going to the doctor the same way I treat being around you. I'm nervous I won't like what you'll say to me, so I don't talk at all.

I grew up in the perfect family. That didn't last for long. Maybe I'm overthinking this all. The social anxiety, the obsession with people being proud of me. Maybe I can just blame it all on being homeschooled. It does seem to explain a lot. My parents taught me a lot of things, and I love and respect them in so many ways, but even they'll admit they never taught me how to have an honest conversation. And I'm not talking about lying, but how I only ever speak in half-truths. I learned to have integrity, but never how to be vulnerable with people. And they loved me for it. I don't know who *they* are, some amalgamation of all the people who've praised me for being a smart, young man.

She's pretty and funny. I would tell her, but what if she finds me weird? I have another friend who I want to hang out with. What if they're too busy for me? Lately, I've been feeling anxious, a little unwell at times. I'll never admit it though, because what would my family and friends think of me if they knew?

The lady sitting next to me said her family wasn't the type to have real conversations about things. Reality often breaks our illusion, after all. She never said anything about going to church, but I'm sure she grew up spending Sundays in a pew just like me. I still hold onto the notion that love is earned. I'm afraid to break the illusion, because then people won't want me around anymore. I fear that they will tell me to shut up, so I never give them a reason to. Why am I giving this insecurity of mine the satisfaction? Do I really think that constant half-truths are substantial? All anyone will ever see is half a person. And that's fifty percent too little for me. I want to make a fool of myself. I want to tell my friend I think she's cute, because she is. I want to stop caring what *they* will think.

Hey, guess what? My family was never perfect. I was never perfect. I'm not some mature, patient, talented prodigy. Behind the mask I'm a skinny, slightly self-obsessed, anxious writer. Hopelessly in love, hopeful in my beliefs. I'm just patient enough to teach a kid how to do a side kick, but I'm overeager for everything else. I'm well-spoken, well just you wait till you hear the things I decided not to say. I'm crazy. I like to think in the best ways. I've been so obsessed with this perfect illusion of myself, that I miss the things that make me human. I don't need to be made of gold for people to find worth in me.

To the lady next to me, I apologize for eavesdropping on your conversation. I hope you have a good rest of your day. And to the person reading this, I would apologize for bothering you with my rambling, but if you're still reading at this point, I probably shouldn't feel that sorry. Thank you for listening.

I don't trust therapists.
What kind of human
profits from other
people's misery?
They're the lawyers of
the mind, the psychos of
the psyche.

REAL LIFE FAN FICTION

Real life is boring and sad. It makes me quite mad.
So, I'm going to disregard the facts
and write things the way they should be.

In chapter one, I decide to pick up a guitar
and immediately nail each and every chord.
So, I write a song, and it sounds simply amazing.
Everyone loves it, and they ask me to write another.
"Just you wait," I say. "It's going to be great."

In chapter two, I ask the girl I like out on a date,
and she blushes at how charming I am.
So, we grab dinner and go for a walk.
At the end of the night she says, "We should do this again."
I smile and say to her, "Well, I'm free next Saturday."

In chapter three, I kick so much butt,
that everyone is like, "Hey, that kid is pretty darn good."
So, I take out a few black belts with my spinny kicks
and sweep a dude a foot taller than me off his feet
as I wink and say something clever and quippy.

In chapter four, I write another book,
and the pages start flying off the shelves.
So, I hold a book signing to meet all my adoring fans.
They tell me how much my words have impacted them,
and frankly, I find it all very touching.

In chapter five, I am talking with my girl,
and she tells me how she'll love me no matter what.
So, we talk about life and dreams for a while,
I tear up a bit as I realize she is always here for me,
and I tell her I'll never not be there for her.

In chapter six, I stub my toe on the corner of the couch,
and I try not to scream profanities into the ether.
So, I look the couch in the eyes, or cushions I guess,
and say to it, "How dare you betray me like this."
But it's okay, because every good story needs some drama.

In chapter seven, I celebrate a few birthdays
and start to notice things are changing.
So, I begin to wonder what comes next:
Kids, a house, mild fame, marriage, maybe a degree?
There's so much left to do, and I can't wait for it all.

In chapter eight, I am all grown up
and I think to myself I've had a pretty lucky life.
So, every day I look for ways to give back to the world.
My way of saying thanks for everything being so great.
It's my turn to make someone else smile.

In chapter nine, I have a little talk with God
as I wonder why my story went the way it did.
So, while waiting for a response, I begin thinking.
Was this the result of hard work or something more?
God or random chance? Maybe it was a mix of both.

In chapter ten, I sit down to write a little story
about change, love, creativity, inspiration, and family.
So, I open a new tab on my computer screen.
I type a few words, then shake my head and erase them.
I do this for a couple hours, unable to write anything.

Eventually, I just smile and close my computer.
I walk back into the living room,
where my favorite people are waiting for me.
We eat dinner together and go for a walk around town.
In the end I know there's no story I could write
that would ever be better than real life.

Keep Fighting

Life has this funny habit of just when you think you have it all figured out, wreaking everything with a storm. Even if it's the middle of November. The things I thought I knew make no sense to me now. I said I was going to leave it all behind, all the pain, all the nonsense, but I paused once I stepped my right foot out the door. I've been walking in all directions, and I don't understand what it means. I'm not even sure who I am anymore, and I mean that in a more literal sense than you may realize. Things have been crazy, when are they not? All year I've been chasing something shiny, disregarding where it's led me. Distracted by something pretty in more ways than one.

I worked myself till I was sick. Confronted by a cold front, now I'm wearing multiple layers and still shaking. Sniffling while I write, overheating while I teach. I used to sleep just fine, but anymore I can't make it through the night in one go. I wonder if I would be happier if I knew less about myself. They say ignorance is bliss but look where ignorance got us. I just turned on the news to see that our leaders are assembling a super team of the worst people you know. And I have to just keep going, act like that's okay. Pretend to be normal.

I could leave. Why bother fighting a fight you'll only lose? I can't change the people I'm not, and I won't become the person I'm not. Life has this funny habit of contradicting itself with a rhyme. Like in the funny way I always think I'm running out of time. The closer I get to running away, the more I want to stay and fight. I can never just make up my mind. But I've also never felt so happy in a place I swear I'm trapped in.

Every time I pray I walk right back over my own words, then try to apologize for the constant rambling. Why do I spend so much time saying sorry for being who I am? I said I was going to leave it all behind, but I still haven't. And honestly, I don't want to. Instead, I want to take the best parts of life and hold them as close as possible. Feel their warmth even when it gets cold. I won't apologize for that. Things have been crazy, we all know that much, but so what? I'm not going to let that stop me from believing in life, I only get one after all. Just the same, I believe in you. And I want to believe that you love me too.

I've always told my kids that when you get knocked down you have to stand back up. When the bullies punch you in the face you punch them back. When life takes you down you can't just stay on the ground. Hey kid, we're about to have to stand back up a lot. We're going to get knocked down again and again and again. It's starting to feel like I should just lie down and take it. Just accept fate. But no. I've never been one to back down or run away. Because I'm a fighter. And I'm going to keep fighting. Even when I'm bruised and sore, I'm going to keep fighting. Even when it hurts to get out of bed, I'm going to keep going. Because that's what I do. I keep fighting.

Nothing and no one are going to stop me from living life. No villain will keep me down. No fear is going to stop me from falling in love. No friend will prevent me from being honest. And I truly do believe, I believe that no storm will ever stop me.